SHORT CIRCULAR WALKS
AROUND
MATLOCK

JOHN N
(Foo

Maps and photographs by John N. Merrill.

a J.N.M. PUBLICATION

1992

a J.N.M. PUBLICATION,

J.N.M. PUBLICATIONS,
WINSTER,
MATLOCK,
DERBYSHIRE.
DE4 2DQ
☎ Winster (0629) 650454
FAX Winster (0629) 650416

Edited, typeset, designed, paged, marketed and distributed by John N. Merrill.

© Text and routes - John N. Merrill 1992.

© Maps and photographs - John N. Merrill 1992.

First Published - July 1985
Reprinted in 1987 and 1989.
This edition - January 1992

ISBN 0 907496 56 3

Meticulous research has been undertaken to ensure that this publication is highly accurate at the time of going to press. The publishers, however, cannot be held responsible for alterations, errors or omissions, but they would welcome notification of such for future editions.

Typeset in - Eagle book and bold and Plantin - bold, italic and plain 9pt and 18pt.

Printed by - John N. Merrill at Milne House, Speedwell Mill, Miller's Green, Wirksworth, Derbyshire. DE4 4BL

Cover sketch by John Creber - "Victoria Tower, Heights of Abraham" - © J.N.M. PUBLICATIONS 1992.

An all British product.

**Hi!
- a few notes
about
Footslogger.**

He was born in the flatlands around Luton in Bedfordshire, but his athletic capabilities soon showed themselves on Sports Day and in the football and cricket teams. Although expelled twice from different schools, he moved to Sheffield and was taken out into the Peak District at the age of 6 1/2. Here he ran up and down the rocks and the sense of enjoyment and freedom has never left him. He was hooked on the outdoors for life. By the age of 15 he had 350 books on the Himalayas and other mountain areas and although failed all eight O levels, he was writing a book on the history of mountaineering! At 16 he soloed the 90 foot high school building and the headmaster rushed him off to Outward Bound Mountain School to be properly trained - he thought it was a fantastic holiday!

At 17 he was chosen with eleven others to go on an expedition to Norway, for a month. Since then he has walked more than 150,000 miles in different parts of the world. He has walked The Cleveland Way 8 times; The Peakland Way 14 times; The Limey Way 14 times; The Pennine Way 4 times; Offa's Dyke 3 times; Pembrokeshire Coast Path 3 times; and all the other official paths at least twice.

He is an avid walker and never known to be really tired; likes to carry heavy loads at 18,000 feet and hates having his socks or shirts washed after a six month walk! His ideal day is a 25 mile walk with three bars of chocolate in his pocket. Having worn out nearly fifty pairs of boots he truly lives upto his nickname, Footslogger!

Stile near Flatts Farm.

CONTENTS

INTRODUCTION

Matlock lies just outside the Peak District National Park, but is surrounded by a wealth of places of interest amidst beautiful walking countryside. These short circular walks of about four miles each bring you to all the principal places of interest in the area. In the north is Darley Dale and its church with 2,000 year old yew tree. Close by are extensive mill ponds, the remains of former industries; while opposite is the solitary tree on the crest of Oaker Hill mingled with various legends.

Moving towards Matlock is a delightful walk beside the River Derwent, before various walks explore 'The Matlocks'. One traces Matlock's industrial past and line of former cable car route. Another ascends the slopes to Riber Castle and its extensive viewpoint and fauna reserve. Opposite a walk crosses the fields to Bonsall and its remarkable thirteen-stepped cross. Perhaps the most unusual walk of all starts from Matlock over the limestone cliff of High Tor before taking the cable car to the summit of the Heights of Abraham. You return along tracks and fields back to downtown Matlock.

To the south you explore the industrial genius of Sir Richard Arkwright, who at Cromford started his cotton spinning empire and the factory system we know today. Close by you walk along a canal and ascend a former railway line and explore a rugged gritstone outcrop — the Black Rocks of Cromford. The most southern walk links four villages together, with the famous Lea Rhododendron Gardens and Dethick, the former home of Sir Anthony Babington, who was later executed for his part in the Babington Plot to rescue Mary, Queen of Scots. In the final stages you pass Lea Hurst, the former home of Florence Nightingale — "The Lady with the Lamp".

As you can see, Matlock is an extremely interesting area to walk in, providing walks to get some exercise while learning and exploring the area. I hope you enjoy walking the area as much as I do.

Happy walking,

JOHN N. MERRILL.

ABOUT THE WALKS -

Whilst every care is taken detailing and describing the walks in this book, it should be borne in mind that the countryside changes by the seasons and the work of man. I have described the walks to the best of my ability, detailing what I have found on the walk in the way of stiles and signs. Obviously with the passage of time stiles become broken or replaced by a ladder stile or even a small gate. Signs too have a habit of being broken or pushed over. All the routes follow rights of way and only on rare occasions will you have to overcome obstacles in its path, such as a barbed wire fence or electric fence.

The seasons bring occasional problems whilst out walking which should also be borne in mind. In the height of summer paths become overgrown and you will have to fight your way through in a few places. In low lying areas the fields are often full of crops, and although the pathline goes straight across it may be more practical to walk round the field edge to get to the next stile or gate. In summer the ground is generally dry but in autumn and winter, especially because of our climate, the surface can be decidedly wet and slippery; sometimes even glutonous mud!

1

Crown Square, Matlock.

ABOUT MATLOCK —

Matlock or rather The Matlocks, as this encompasses several villages — Matlock Green, Matlock Bath, Matlock Bridge — is strung along the banks of the River Derwent and dominated by stunning limestone scenery. It is only in the last 160 years that the town has become a major tourist resort, with its fame initially coming from its spa era. The first spring was discovered in 1698, another in 1735 known as the New Bath, and today's hotel has an indoor plunge pool and outdoor pool fed by the thermal water. The water has a constant temperature of 20c (68F). By 1838 Matlock Bath was becoming a fashionable spa, with regular coach traffic and notable visitors in Lord Byron and Ruskin. The nearby village of Cromford was the scene of Sir Richard Arkwright's cotton spinning empire.

Many of the major buildings on Matlock Bank date from Victorian times and were built as hydropathic establishments. The County offices were originally Smedley's hydro. Running up Bank Road to it was a cable tramway, like the San Francisco ones, but it ceased operating in 1927. Today the area is a popular tourist base for the Peak District National Park, with numerous places to visit in the area. The River Derwent is a popular boating area in Matlock Bath, and the bankside is illuminated in the early autumn. Lead mining dates back to Roman times and these mines can be explored and the area viewed from High Tor or the Heights of Abraham, reached by cable car.

Early Closing day — Thursday

Market Days — Tuesday and Friday

Tourist Information Office — The Pavilion, Matlock Bath. Tel. No. Matlock (0629) 55082

2

WHAT TO SEE/PLACES TO VISIT — a random selection

Riber Castle Wildlife Park — unique collection of British and European birds and animals including the world famous Riber Lynx collection. Tel. Matlock 582073

Heights of Abraham — including cable car, Great Masson Cavern and Great Rutland Cavern — Nestus Mine. Tel.Matlock 582365

High Tor — one of the most impressive viewpoints in the area.

Lead Mining Museum, The Pavilion, Matlock Bath. Tel. Matlock 583834

Guilliver's Kingdom, Matlock Bath — remarkable model village and miniature world. Tel. Matlock 55970.

Arkwright's Cromford Mill — the birthplace of water powered cotton spinning. Tel. Wirksworth **824297**

Tramway Museum, Crich — the most comprehensive collection of trams from around the world. Tel. Ambergate 2565.

Bonsall Church

Darley Dale — 4½ Miles

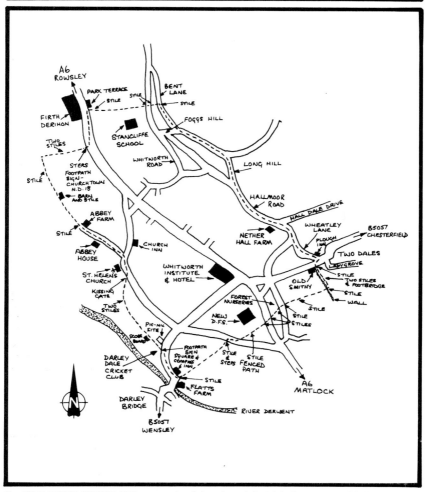

St. HELEN'S CHURCH — much of the church is 14th Century and is believed to have been founded by Edward the Elder in about 900 AD. The tower was built by Sir John de Darley, whose recumbent effigy is inside. He was for a while the Governor of Peak Castle — Peveril Castle at Castleton. Near the entrance is the Whitworth Pew and memorial window to Sir Joseph Whitworth. He is synonymous with Darley Dale, being responsible for much of the building nearby, the Whitworth Institute, and Stancliffe Hall; now a Boys' School. Among his many engineering achievements, he was the inventor of the Whitworth thread.

Other items of interest are the 16th Century Rollesley Monuments and the 17th Century Polyglot Brass.

The yew tree is more than 2,000 years old, and four feet above the ground has a girth of 33 feet.

4

DARLEY DALE — 4½ Miles
Allow 2½ hours

CAR PARK — Darley Dale Picnic Site.

MAPS — O.S. 1:25,000 Outdoor Leisure Map — The White Peak — East Sheet
O.S. 1:25,000 Pathfinder Series — Bakewell and Matlock —
Sheet SK 26/36

ABOUT THE WALK — First you cross the fields to Churchtown and see one of
the oldest churches in Derbyshire and a 2,000 year old yew tree. Next you walk along
the valley floor before beginning to encircle the Darley Dale area, on good paths and
country lanes. The views are extensive from Darley Hillside. Close by you can
extend the walk by three miles and explore the woodland of Hall Dale — this makes
an excellent walk in its own right and is detailed separately (see Hall Dale walk).
Finally you descend to Two Dales and cross the fields back to Darley Bridge.

WALKING INSTRUCTIONS — Turn right out of the picnic site and right again,
as footpath signposted, and walk along beside the cricket ground. At the score board
leave the track for the stile and keep to the righthand edge of the field to the next
stile. Cross the next diagonally to another stile, before passing a house garden on
your right to gain a kissing gate and Church Lane. Turn left, passing the church on
your left. Just beyond, bear left along the 'No Through Road', passing the school on
your left and walking along the drive of Abbey House. Follow the drive onto a track
with Abbey Farm on your right. At the end of the track ascend the stile and keep the
wall on your right to the next stile beside a barn. Keep ahead across to the next stile.
50 yards beyond, turn right through a large gap in the hedge (the actual stile is on the
left but overgrown). Reach the dismantled railway line and cross it and via two stiles.
Ascend the field beyond to the A6 road — steps, stile and path sign — Churchtown
ND18.

Turn left along the A6 road for 100 yards. Just before the bus stop and Park Terrace,
turn right up the track to a stile. Continue ascending up the field to a stile and
Whitworth Road. Cross to the next stile and ascend to Bent Lane. Turn right and
walk along the lane, bearing left at the junction with Foggs Hill. Upon reaching
Long Hill, turn right down this, passing Hallmoor on your left. At the bottom turn
left along Hallmoor Road. Just over ¼ mile along here is the drive and footpath for
Hall Dale. (If you do the three-mile circuit up here you will return to the same place
). Continue along Hallmoor Road, now descending. At Wheatley House, bear left
and descend Wheatley Road, reaching Two Dales and the Plough Inn on your left.
Turn right to the B5057 road. Cross to your left to the stile on the left of the Old
Smithy. Follow the tarmaced path across Warney Brook, 40 yards later turn right
through the stile and cross the field to another stile. Just beyond you reach another
tarmaced path, which you follow to the road beside Forest Nurseries. Cross the road
to another stile and keep on the fenced path to the A6 road. Again cross the road to a
stile on your left, and, keeping the field boundary on your left, you reach the next
stile and slab bridge. On your right is the 'New DFS'. At the road turn right, and just
over the railway bridge on your left is the path sign, stile and gritstone steps. Cross
the field beyond to the road — B5057 — with the Square and Compass Inn on your
right and Flatts Farm on your left. Turn right back to the car park and picnic site.

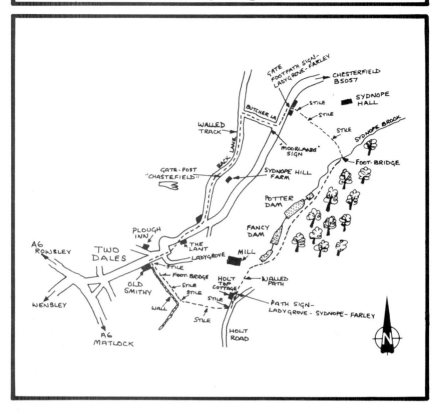

GATEPOST — At the entrance to Sydnope Hill Farm can be seen a guidepost, now used as a gatepost. On one side can be seen the word "Chastefield" and pointing hand. Two Dales was a welcome sight for early travellers who had crossed the moors from Chesterfield. Sydnope Hill was particularly arduous, and the new road is little better. In the Plough Inn area were four inns, and the Smithy was close by.

THE HOLT — Both Ladygrove House and The Holt were built by the Dakeynes family. The Dakeynes moved here from Snitterton in the 16th Century. Ladygrove House was built in 1796, and The Holt's basement was used as a bank until 1881.

TWO DALES — was formerly known as Toadhole until the late 19th Century. The name Two Dales is the most apt, as the village lies at the base of two dales — Hall Dale on the left and the Sydnope valley on the right.

TWO DALES & SYDNOPE — 4 Miles
Allow 2 hours

CAR PARK — No official one in Two Dales, but parking room beside B5057.

MAPS — O.S. 1:25,000 Outdoor Leisure Map — The White Peak — East Sheet O.S. 1:25,000 Pathfinder Series — Bakewell and Matlock — Sheet SK 26/36

ABOUT THE WALK — Two Dales has several interesting buildings and a large mill. On this walk you pass several fine buildings, and obtain a grand view of the village and mill, before ascending past the mill pond to the summit of Sydnope Hill. You return via an old road providing distant views of the area and Hall Dale on your right. There is no inn on the route — just one close to the start or end of your walk!

WALKING INSTRUCTIONS — Start the walk on the B5057 road in Two Dales, approximately opposite the side road leading to the Plough Inn. The path and stile are on the immediate left of the house — The Old Smithy. The path is tarmaced as you first cross a field with the wall on your righthand side. Cross a footbridge and begin ascending gently. At the third stile the wall on your right and tarmaced path bear right. You ascend to your left to a stile and ascend the field beyond to Holt Road. Turn left, and 30 yards later beside Holt Top Cottage and as signposted — Ladygrove, Sydnope and Farley — bear left and descend the walled path. At the bottom keep right and follow the well-defined path above the mill ponds on your left. You keep on this path for almost a mile, passing Fancy Dam and Potter Dam. Beyond the path becomes little used, but keep close to the brook to reach the footbridge.

Cross the bridge and ascend the slope ahead. Just over the brow you reach a stile. Continue across the next field to another stile. Far to your right is Sydnope Hall. As directed, cross the fenced path, at the end of which is a wooden door onto the B5057 road. Turn left, and 50 yards later turn right onto the lane, signposted for 'Moorlands'. At the T-junction beyond, turn left onto a walled track and keep on this for just over ½ mile. Partway down on your left is the entrance to Sydnope Hill Farm. The righthand gatepost is a guide post. On joining the B5057 road again turn right and continue descending. Where the road turns sharp right, keep ahead and descend the path on the right of the house, "The Lant". At the bottom follow the B5057 road on your right, back to your starting point.

TWO DALES MILL — In 1785 a cotton spinning mill was built here. The present building, although considerably enlarged by the present owners — S. and E. Johnson (East) Ltd. — dates from 1826 and was built by the Dakeyne family for flax spinning. The dams provided a 96 ft. head of water, and the large water pipes on the original building fed water to the hydraulic engine which powered the machines. The Dakeynes in 1830 patented a special disc engine for this.

Hall Dale — 3 Miles

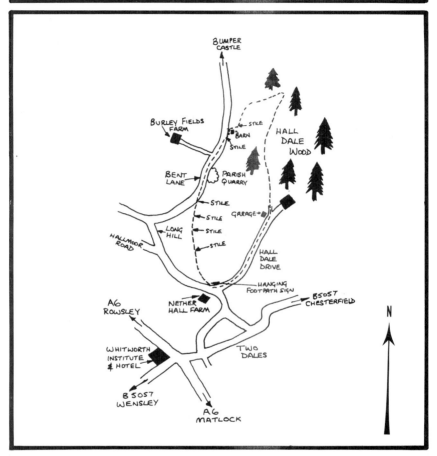

River Derwent near Oaker.

8

HALL DALE — 3 Miles
Allow 1½ hours

MAPS — O.S. 1:25,000 Outdoor Leisure Map — The White Peak — East Sheet
O.S. 1:25,000 Pathfinder Series — Bakewell and Matlock —
Sheet SK 26/36

ABOUT THE WALK — A short but really delightful walk. There is no car park,
but parking is possible at its northern end. The walk can either be done in its own
right or as an extension to the Darley Dale circuit.

WALKING INSTRUCTIONS — At the entrance of Hall Dale Lane on Hallmoor
Road, opposite the entrance to Nether Hall Farm, walk up the driveway, as footpath
signposted. Keep on the drive for almost ½ a mile. At the entrance to the house, with
garages on your left, bear left onto a track, signposted 'Public Footpath'. Keep on
this well-defined path for just over ½ a mile. Turn left on distinct path up a shallow
depression. The path curves to your left, and at the top is close to the forest's
perimeter. After ¼ mile turn right through the stile by the gate and cross the field
beside a wall to a barn. Turn left beyond it to reach a stile on your right and the road.
Turn left and descend the road, passing the entrance to Burley Fields Farm on your
right and a small quarry on your left. Just afterwards, where the road turns right, on
your left is the footpath stile. Begin descending the fields, keeping the wall on your
right, and reaching the stile as you do so. After ¼ mile reach the wood and stile.
Continue descending on a wide path, keeping ahead at all cross paths. In the final
stages the path bears left to the entrance of Hall Dale Lane, where you began.

Square & Compass Inn — Darley Bridge.

Three Villages — 4½ Miles

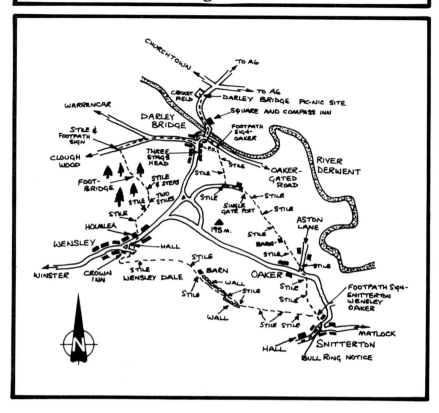

OAKER HILL — Near the summit stands a solitary tree. Although a single tree is described in a poem by William Wordsworth, the tree was planted in 1911 to honour King George V's coronation. There are several legends about the tree — the most popular one concerning two brothers. Both ascended the hill and planted a tree before going their separate ways. The one who did well — the tree grew and flourised. The one who failed — his tree withered and died.

SNITTERTON HALL — An excellent example of an Elizabethan Manor house. Believed to have been built in 1631 by John Milward.

BULL RING — The stone plaque records the location of the bull ring — 22 feet away. Bull baiting was one of the highlights of Wakes and fairs. Before baiting began with bull dogs, the bull's horns were protected and the bull secured to either a stake or ring. The sport was abolished by law in 1835.

THREE VILLAGES — 4½ Miles
Allow 2 hours

CAR PARK — Darley Bridge picnic site.

MAPS — O.S. 1:25,000 Outdoor Leisure Map — The White Peak — East Sheet
O.S. 1:25,000 Pathfinder Series — Bakewell and Matlock —
Sheet SK 26/36

ABOUT THE WALK — A walk that has a little of everything — river and field
walking, impressive vantage points, dale walking and pine forest. En route you pass
close to three small villages rich in architecture and pass three inns. The view from
near Oaker over Matlock and Darley Dale is stunning. A short extension will bring
you into Snitterton to see its Hall and Bull Ring notice.

WALKING INSTRUCTIONS — Turn right out of the car park along the road to
Darley Bridge. On your right is the Darley Dale Cricket Club ground, whose Club
was founded in 1863. Just before crossing the bridge over the River Derwent, on
your left is the Square and Compass Inn. Cross the bridge and turn left onto the
"gated road to Oaker". On your right are the transport firms of Waters and Siddall.
50 yards later turn right, as footpath signed "To Oaker", and cross the field
diagonally to your left, passing a solitary wooden stile before reaching the next. The
path is defined as you walk beside a hedge on your right to another stile and farm
track. Turn left, and just past the farm at a solitary gate post bear right and begin
ascending on a path to another stile. Beyond you walk through a few trees — the path
bears left, then ascends to a stile and rough track. Turn left and follow this to a
vantage point, before descending slightly to your right, with a partially ruined barn
on your right. Keep on the track, and, just past a well trough on your left, go through
the stile and descend the steps and field to a stile near the start of Aston Lane. To
your right are the houses of Oaker.

Walk to the main road and turn left. 30 yards later turn right through the stile and
cross fields to the triple metal footpath sign on the outskirts of Snitterton. Your route
is now to the right — to Wensley. Before walking that way, keep straight ahead into
Snitterton to see the Bull Ring notice stone, and a little up the 'No Through Road' on
your right is Snitterton Hall. Retrace your steps back to the triple sign and left. Cross
the field to a stile in the fence before reaching another one. The next is at the corner
of a wall. Keep the wall on your left to the next stile. From here the wall is now on
your right. At the following stile descend slightly into Wensley Dale. On your right
is a barn with "Footpath to Matlock" in bold white letters. Walk up the dale and,
after the second stile ¼ mile later, turn right and ascend the curving track to
Wensley village. On your left is the Crown Inn. Bear right through the stile to
another close to Wensley Hall on a tarmaced path. Cross the main road to the path
sign — Stanton and Birchover — and walk past Holmlea on the drive, then walled
track. At the second stile, bear right and cross the field to your left to another stile.
Cross the next field to the bottom lefthand corner to two stiles, and enter the pine
plantation. Keep on the well-defined path as you descend to a stile and steps before
reaching the footbridge, three minutes later. Ascend through the trees to a field, and
on the opposite side a stile and path sign. Turn right along the road to the junction.
Keep right and descend to Darley Bridge village. Turn left at the junction passing
Potter Cottage, built in 1763, on your right. Reach the Derwent Bridge and retrace
your steps back to the car park.

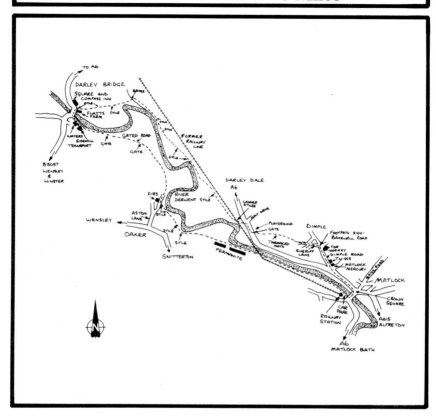

RIVER DERWENT — is the Peak District's and Derbyshire's mightiest river, and almost traverses the county from north to south. The moorland masses of Kinder and Bleaklow, the southern end of the Pennine Way, are its source. South of Derby, between Shardlow and Sawley, the Derwent joins the Trent.

STILES — As you walk this route you reach a wide variety of stiles — from simple wooden ones to magnificent carved stone stiles.

COUNTRYSIDE NOTES —

Birds to be seen — Grey Wagtail, Mallard Ducks, Dipper, Moorhen, Grey Heron, Black Headed Gulls, Coots.

Flowers to be seen — Water forget-me-nots, Water mint, Monkey flower, Water speedwell.

Also — Water shrew and Water vole.

THE RIVER DERWENT — 5 Miles
Allow 2½ hours

CAR PARK — Matlock Bridge, Near Railway Station.

MAPS — O.S. 1:25,000 Outdoor Leisure Map — The White Peak — East Sheet
O.S. 1:25,000 Pathfinder Series — Bakewell and Matlock —
Sheet SK 26/36

ABOUT THE WALK — A delightful level walk along the Derwent valley. First
you walk along the righthand side (western side) of the river to Darley Bridge, where
there is an inn beside the route and halfway point. You return to Matlock along the
lefthand (eastern side) of the river. It is a leisurely stroll along well-defined paths,
giving ample time to admire your surroundings.

WALKING INSTRUCTIONS — In between the Station road and car park,
beside the car park ticket machine, is the tarmaced footpath — signposted "Public
footpath liable to flooding". Follow this path above the river and through the trees,
for a mile. For part of the time on your immediate left is Tarmac's Parmanite works.
Beyond the works you reach a stile. Pass through this and bear right along the
bankside to the next stile. Ahead can be seen the next, after which there is a small
slab footbridge, with a stile at either end. Beyond this ascend to the road, in front of
"Firs" house. Turn right and follow this road which has three gates across before
reaching Darley Dale Bridge a little over a mile away.

Cross the bridge over the Derwent and immediately turn right, passing through the
righthand stile and walking beside Flatts Farm on your right. Before the stile on
your left is the Square and Compass Inn. Keep beside the wall on your left and reach
some of the finest stiles to be seen anywhere. Beyond the third stile you reach the
river again. Bear left over a bridge over a stream and turn right onto a defined path.
You now follow this path, at first beside the river and then away from it, coming to
several stiles and line of the now disused railway line on your left. You cross the fields
guided by the stiles for just over a mile to a ladder stile. Ascend this and cross the line
to another ladder stile and turn right. At the end of the field in the top righthand
corner is a stile and slab over a stream. Cross the next field to a stile and footpath
sign, beside the A6 road. Turn right, and 75 yards later left, through the gates, and
ascend the paved then tarmaced path on the right of a playground. Keep on this path
for ½ mile, crossing two roads and with the housing estate on your immediate right.
At the top come into Sheriff Lane, and at the junction with Dimple Road see a
footpath sign — Bakewell Road — on your right. Turn and descend Dimple Road to
the A6 road beside Twigg's and the Matlock Mercury office on your left. Turn left to
Crown Square, where turn right over Matlock Bridge back to the car park, on your
right.

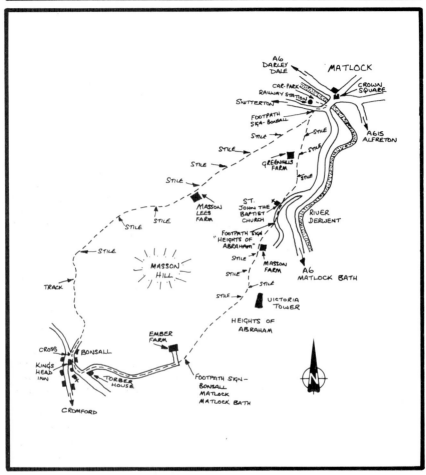

Bonsall Cross & King's Head Inn.

BONSALL — The village observes the well-dressing ceremony each year in early August. The Cross was built in 1671 and the King's Head Inn in 1677 — a beam in the bar has "1677 Anthony Abell". The Church dates from the 13th Century.

BONSALL — 5 Miles
Allow 2½ hours

CAR PARK — Matlock Bridge, Near Railway Station.

MAPS — O.S. 1:25,000 Outdoor Leisure Map — The White Peak — East Sheet
O.S. 1:25,000 Pathfinder Series — Bakewell and Matlock —
Sheet SK 26/36
O.S. 1:25,000 Pathfinder Series — Matlock (South) —
Sheet SK 25/35

ABOUT THE WALK — First you ascend out of Matlock, with distant views over the town behind. You ascend fields over the limestone plateau before descending to the former lead-mining village of Bonsall, complete with thirteen-stepped cross and a 17th Century inn. To return to Matlock you ascend past Bonsall Church and follow a defined path to the Heights of Abraham. You follow further paths and tracks providing views over to High Tor, before rejoining your starting-out path.

WALKING INSTRUCTIONS — Return to the A6 road and turn right and right again immediately afterwards up Snitterton Road, passing The Royal Bank of Scotland on your right and a flower shop on your left. Just beyond, at the entrance to Bridge Farm, turn left onto the signposted path — Bonsall. After a few yards you reach an open field, which you ascend directly on a well- defined path — on your return you regain this field in the middle and retrace your steps. At the end cross a lane, passing a footpath sign — "Bonsall via Masson Hill 1½ miles". Continue on the defined path, keeping the field boundary on your left. Pass through several stiles before approaching Masson Lees Farm, ½ mile away. Pass it on your right, and at the top of the field is a stile and track beyond. Turn right, and after 20 yards bear left, gently ascending around the fringe of a quarry to a stile and another shortly afterwards before a track. Turn right down the track for 20 yards to a stile on your left. Cross the field to a gap before walking between two widely-spaced walls for two fields. Pass through two stiles before bearing right to a track; turn left along this. At first it is simply a grassed track. Later it becomes walled, and, as you near Bonsall, a concrete walkway. After ¼ mile bear left on the track and follow it all the way to Bonsall, entering the village opposite the Cross and King's Head Inn.

Turn left and ascend Church Street, passing the church on your right. Immediately afterwards, beside Torber House, turn left and ascend the lane, which soon swings to your right. Little over ¼ mile later, the track turns sharp left to Ember Farm. Keep straight ahead to triple footpath sign. Turn left, following the "Matlock" path. This well-defined path weaves its way through woodland before descending to the fence of the Heights of Abraham. Bear left to a stile, and continue descending gradually to the lefthand side of Masson Farm. Just beyond you bear right and descend to a track and path sign — "Heights of Abraham". Turn left along the descending track, and 100 yards later pass St. John's Chapel on your left. Immediately afterwards turn left onto a walled path, and keep on this defined path as it contours round. Opposite Greenhills Farm, pass through two stiles on your right and begin crossing the fields to your right to regain your first field. Turn right and retrace your steps back to Matlock Bridge.

Matlock's Alpine Walk — 5 Miles

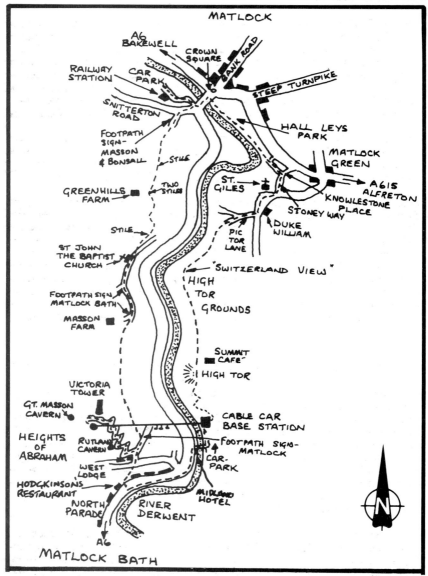

CAR PARK — Matlock Bridge, Near Railway Station.

MAPS — O.S. 1:25,000 Outdoor Leisure Map — The White Peak — East Sheet
O.S. 1:25,000 Pathfinder Series — Bakewell and Matlock —
Sheet SK 26/36
O.S. 1:25,000 Pathfinder Series — Matlock (South) —
Sheet SK 25/35

MATLOCK'S ALPINE WALK — 5 Miles
Allow 3 hours

ABOUT THE WALK — Lord Byron wrote about the area — "There are prospects in Derbyshire as noble as any in Greece or Switzerland." This walk has an alpine feel to it, with a "Switzerland View" — high rocky outcrops with dizzily steep faces to the River Derwent hundreds of feet below, and a cable car ascent. The walk is perhaps the most expensive to make, with an entry admission to High Tor Grounds and cable car ride. But I would suggest it is perhaps one of the more unusual walks to be made in the area — if not in Britain. There is plenty to see en route, and a very full afternoon can be had if you visit the caverns of High Tor and Heights of Abraham.

THE CABLE CAR — a charge is made for the ride to the Heights and operates from Easter to end of October. The 1989 charges are — Adults £3.75 and children £1.99. Outside the operating times or in strong winds when it might be closed or for those not wishing to take the cable car you can reach West Lodge on foot by —

Descending past the Cable Car Base Station and walking under the railway bridge. Turn left along the track with the River Derwent on your right. At the end bear right to the A6 road beside the Midland Hotel on your left. Turn left along A6 road and walk along North Parade with the River on your left for almost ¼ mile. Just past the Post Office turn right up Waterloo Road; infront of Hodgkinson's Restaurant. A short distance up here, opposite the Coach House and as signposted — Heights of Abraham — turn left and ascend the cobbled path. Cross a road and continue ascending the cobbled path which later becomes tarmaced. At the top gain West Lodge. Turn right down the road for a few yards and turn left onto the footpath signposted Matlock — as detailed in the second paragraph of the walking instructions.

WALKING INSTRUCTIONS — Walk to the A6 road and turn left and cross the road bridge over the River Derwent. Turn right immediately afterwards and walk through Hall Leys Park. At the end continue ahead along Knowlestone Place. Turn right at the first road on your right — Stoney Way — which is a 'No Through Road'. At the top turn right, passing St. Giles' Church on your right and the Duke William Inn on your left. Just beyond the inn turn right into Pic Tor Lane. 75 yards down here turn left into High Tor Grounds. A small admission charge is made here. Ascend the well-defined track to the Summit Cafe, passing en route the impressive Switzerland View. At the other side of the Cafe begin descending down a zig-zag path, with the cliff edge on your right. The path is steep in a few places. At the bottom you reach the Cable Car Base Station. Catch the next cable car to the Heights of Abraham — a charge is made.

After your visit descend the zig-zag pathway down the slope to Great Rutland Cavern and West Lodge. Turn left, and 75 yards later turn left again, as footpath signposted — "Matlock" — and ascend the fenced path. First you ascend before contouring round underneath the cable car line and through woodland to the entrance to Masson Farm. Continue ahead on the track to a small road with a Matlock Bath footpath sign. Descend the road to just below St. John the Baptist Chapel, and turn left onto a footpath, with wall on right. Approximately a third of a mile later, with Greenhills Farm on your left, pass through one stile and another immediately afterwards on your right. Cross the next field to another stile before bearing right and descending to Snitterton Road. Turn right, and 50 yards later reach the A6 road and Matlock Bridge just ahead. Turn left into the car park.

St. Giles Church, Matlock.

MATLOCK PARISH CHURCH — dedicated to St. Giles. The original church was Norman, but the present has a 15th Century perpendicular tower and the rest is 19th Century. The gravestones are well worth looking at, while inside is the Woolley Tomb. Adam Woolley died in 1657 aged 100, and his wife, Grace, died in 1669 aged 110. They were married for 76 years, and lived at Riber Hall. Close by are a collection of Crantses (Maidens' Garlands) in a glass case. When an unmarried girl died before her wedding, a paper garland was made and carried in front of her coffin. At the end of the proceedings it was hung above the deceased's person's pew. The font is 13th Century.

High Tor

HIGH TOR — The summit is 600 feet above sea level and the limestone face drops sheer to the River Derwent, 396 feet below. The face has numerous rock climbing routes. Two lead mines, now known as caves — Roman Cave and Fern Cave — can be explored.

18

Cable Car — Heights of Abraham

CABLE CAR — Built during the winter of 1983/4, and opened for Easter in 1984 at a cost of £750,000. the cable car operates from Easter to end of October and whisks you within minutes to the Heights of Abraham; en route is a stunning view of High Tor and the Derwent Valley.

Victoria Tower

HEIGHTS OF ABRAHAM — Named in the 18th Century by an Army Officer who felt they resembled the Heights of Abraham at Quebec in Canada. The prominent Victoria Prospect Tower was erected by John Petchill in 1844. The Tree Tops Visitor Centre provides refreshments. Great Masson Cavern and Great Rutland Cavern with Nestus Mine can be explored, and are both former lead mines dating back to Roman times.

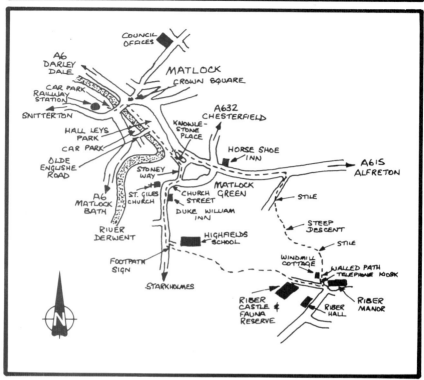

Matlock from Riber Castle

20

RIBER — 3½ Miles
Allow 2 hours

CAR PARK — Matlock Bridge, Near Railway Station.

MAPS — O.S. 1:25,000 Outdoor Leisure Map — The White Peak — East Sheet
O.S. 1:25,000 Pathfinder Series — Bakewell and Matlock —
Sheet SK 26/36
O.S. 1:25,000 Pathfinder Series — Matlock (South) —
Sheet SK 25/35

ABOUT THE WALK — A short walk with a steep ascent to Riber Castle, where a magnificent view of Matlock and the Derwent Valley unfolds. Here you can stop and visit the Fauna Reserve before beginning your descent to Matlock Green. On the walk you can also visit the historic St. Giles Church and see the 17th Century Riber Manor and Hall.

WALKING INSTRUCTIONS — Return to the A6 road and turn left over the Matlock Bridge and right into Hall Leys Park. Keep to the righthand side of the Park, passing the miniature railway on your right. Continue ahead into Knowlestone Place and turn right up the No Through Road — Stoney Way. At the top, as footpath signposted, turn right along the road for ¼ mile for the path to Riber. On your right is St. Giles Church. At the entrance to Highfields School turn left onto the signposted fenced path and follow the defined path past the school before ascending to Riber Castle.

Descend the road from the castle to Riber village. On your left is the Manor, and a little to your right is the Hall. Turn left along the drive to Windmill Cottage, with a telephone kiosk on your right. At the cottage you bear right on a walled path. Beyond the path is defined and well-stiled. Shortly afterwards you descend steeply through trees, then a field, to a stile and walled track. Turn right along this to the A615 road. Turn left to Matlock Green. Pass the Horse Shoe Inn on your right and beyond, just over the brow of the rise, turn left into Knowlestone Place and rejoin your starting out path and trace your footsteps back to the bridge and car park.

RIBER CASTLE — was built between 1862 and 1868 by John Smedley, who had a mill at Lea Bridge and who created the Matlock Hydro, now the County Council Offices in Matlock. The castle is believed to have cost £60,000 to build, and because of the winter gales has no doorway on its northern side. In the 1920s it was a school, and since the 1960s has been a Fauna Reserve, housing one of the finest collections of British and European wildlife in Britain.

RIBER MANOR — mostly dates from 1633, but some parts are of earlier construction.

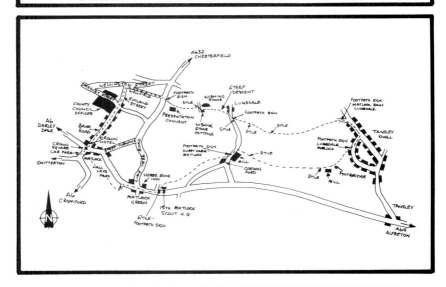

Wishing Stone

MATLOCK'S CABLE TRAMWAY — Running from Crown Square to the top of Rutland Street was this tramway, opened in 1893 and closed 34 years later in 1927. It was the steepest tramway in the world, climbing 300 feet in half a mile. The fare was "tuppence up the bank and a penny down".

WISHING STONE — According to local tradition, you should sit on the stone and wish; and your wish would come true!

LUMSDALE — Lead mining in the area dates from Roman times, and in the 18th Century there were numerous lead-smelting mills in the neighbourhood. Today only the shell of the buildings remain.

MATLOCK'S INDUSTRIAL PAST — 5 Miles
Allow 2½ hours

CAR PARK — Matlock Bridge, Near Railway Station.

MAPS — O.S. 1:25,000 Outdoor Leisure Map — The White Peak — East Sheet
O.S. 1:25,000 Pathfinder Series — Bakewell and Matlock —
Sheet SK 26/36
O.S. 1:25,000 Pathfinder Series — Matlock (South) —
Sheet SK 25/35

ABOUT THE WALK — First you ascend the steep Bank Road, tracing the line of Matlock's tramway route; similar to that running in San Francisco today. Next you maintain your height to pass the legendary Wishing Stone, before descending steeply down to the ruins of the lead-smelting miles at Lumsdale. Field walking brings you to Tansley, where you head back to Matlock, passing further mills and mill ponds.

WALKING INSTRUCTIONS — Return to the A6 road and turn left, and cross the River Derwent to Crown Square. Cross over to Bank Road, inbetween the Crown Hotel and the Wine House, and begin your ascent. At the top of Bank Road with the County Council Offices on your left, continue ascending Rutland Street, passing the tramway engine house on your left. Just above and before Wellington Street, turn right onto the narrow lane — Wellfield — and walk past the houses; later it is just a path with allotments on your right. Later it becomes a road as you gain the Chesterfield Road. As footpath-signposted cross over to a stile and path and follow this to a road, which takes you past the Presentation Convent on your right. Shortly afterwards the road bears right to a farm; you keep left on a walled path. At the top turn right and left 20 yards later, passing Wishing Stone Cottage on your right. Continue past the houses into open country with the large Wishing Stone on your left. Continue ahead and descend the steep well-defined cobbled path to Lumsdale Road.

Cross over to your right to a stile and footpath sign. Follow this defined path as you pass a ruin on your right in the second field. The stiles will guide you to a track, which you follow to the road and houses of Tansley Knoll. A footpath sign here indicates — Matlock Bath and Lumsdale. Turn right and swing to your left on the path which soon passes a mill pond on your right. Shortly afterwards cross a footbridge, bearing right. Upon reaching another path with the mill building on your left, turn right and follow this fenced and walled path, which gradually bears right across the fields and is tarmaced. In ¼ of a mile you reach the Lumsdale Road and mill buildings on your left. Turn left, and 100 yards later and just in front of Gordon Fords buildings turn right, as footpath-signposted — Hurst Farm Estate and Matlock. Follow the path around the factory, keeping left and passing a playing field on your right. The path is well-defined and tarmaced much of the way. Pass another mill on your left and keep ahead on the path, eventually reaching the A615 road, close to Matlock Green, with the 15th Matlock Scout H.Q. on your left. Turn right and walk towards Matlock, passing the Horse Shoe Inn on your right. Just over the brow of the rise turn left into Hall Leys Park and pass the tennis courts to regain Matlock Bridge and car park.

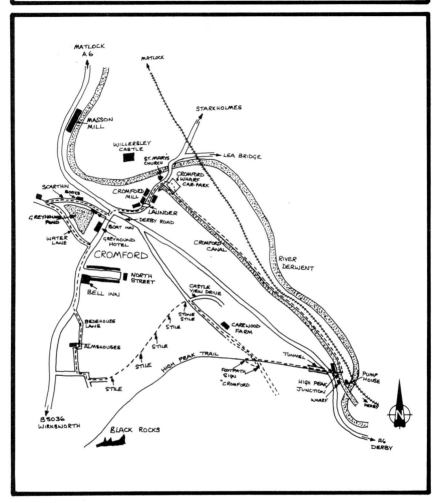

LEAWOOD PUMP HOUSE — To maintain the water level in the canal, this pump house was built in 1840 to pump water from the River Derwent. Inside is the original Graham and Co. beam engine. When operating, it can lift between 5 and 6 tons of water a minute. Nearby is the aqueduct over the River Derwent.

HIGH PEAK JUNCTION — To link the Cromford Canal with the Peak Forest Canal at Whaley Bridge, a canal was proposed, but, because of the hilly terrain of the Peak District it was not practical. Instead, a railway with nine inclines was built and operating in 1831. The 33-mile journey took two days, and up each incline the wagons had to be hauled. It was never a viable railway, and the last section closed in 1967. Since then a 17- mile section from here to Dowlow near Buxton has been converted to a pedestrian way. The incline you ascend is known as the Cromford Incline and is 580 yards long and a 1 in 9 gradient.

CROMFORD VILLAGE WALK — 3 Miles
Allow 2 hours

MAPS — O.S. 1:25,000 Outdoor Leisure series — The White Peak — East Sheet — O.S. 1:25,000 Pathfinder Series Sheet No. SK25/35 — Matlock South.

CAR PARK — Cromford Wharf

Early Closing Day — Thursday

ABOUT THE WALK — In 1771 Richard Arkwright started a cotton spinning mill here which led to a huge industry in Derbyshire and the Midlands. He developed the factory system, and is today known as "The Father of the Factory System". On this walk you see at first hand much of his original buildings — mills and workers' houses — while walking beside a canal and ascending a unique railway line; now a pedestrian way. You pass several inns; can visit Arkwright's original mill; and go for a boat trip on the canal in the summer months.

WALKING INSTRUCTIONS — From the car park walk up to the canal, turn left and follow the tow path to the High Peak Junction, just over a mile away. Cross the bridge and begin ascending the High Peak Trail, passing through a tunnel under the A6 road. Before crossing the canal you can extend the walk a short distance to see the wharf and Pump House. Ascend the trail for a third of a mile, and, shortly after passing a small building on your right, you reach a path sign on your left — "Cromford". Leave the trail and follow the path past and walk through the tunnel under the trail, following a walled path for the next ½ mile.

Pass Carrwood Farm on your right and enter a housing estate. Just before Castle View Drive on your right, leave the road and follow the distinct stiled path on your left for just over ¼ mile. Keep straight ahead on the road and follow it to your right then left. Turn right down Bedehouse Lane, which becomes a tarmaced path in the middle. At the bottom turn right and descend the main road — "Cromford Hill" to central Cromford. On the way you pass North Street on your right.

At the bottom of the hill turn left along Water Lane, and 300 yards later turn right along "Scarthin", on the right of Paul Mark Hairdressers. Turn left at the end to the A6 road. Cross over to the right and descend the road past the original Arkwright Mill to the start of the Cromford Canal and car park.

CROMFORD CANAL — Although opened after his death in 1793, Sir Richard Arkwright had been greatly involved. The canal was 14½ miles long and joined the Erewash Canal at Langley Mill, costing £80,000 to build. The canal enjoyed many years of use until the coming of the railway to Matlock in the 1860s. By 1900 it was closed to through traffic because of the collapse of the Butterley Tunnel. The Cromford Canal Society and Derbyshire County Council have helped to restore this section of the canal. The Society operate boats on the canal and have restored the Leawood Pump House.

North Street

NORTH STREET — Cromford is now a Conservation Area, and much of the housing dates from the late 18th Century, having been built by Sir Richard Arkwright for his workers. These three-storeyed buildings are among the finest examples of industrial archaeology to be found in England. Originally the upper floor of each house was one long room, enabling the family to make stockings.

MILL POND — To feed water to Arkwright's original mill, a series of five mill ponds were constructed — this is the last one. From here the water passes through tunnels and a channel before crossing the road in a cast-iron launder (dated 1821) into the mill.

GREYHOUND HOTEL — Built by Sir Richard Arkwright in 1788. The splendid Georgian front has remained unaltered since then. Close by is the Boat Inn built in 1772.

MASSON MILL — Just along the A6 road and built by Arkwright in 1783. It is still operating today, with more than 200 years of continuous use. The weir is unusual, being convex instead of the normal concave.

WILLERSLEY CASTLE — Sir Richard Arkwright lived in Rock House on the right of the mill, but in 1788 began building his castle. Before work could commence a large boulder was removed at a cost of £3,000. By 1791 the building was almost complete when a fire badly damaged it. Arkwright died the following year and never took up residence.

CROMFORD MILL — Arkwright's original mill, built in 1771. The mill operated almost continuously, with whole families working a twelve hour shift. Arkwright was renowned for his modern thought, and often paid workers when they were ill. In March 1786 he had 480 people working at the mill, with a total wage bill of £95 per week.

Masson Mill

Willersley Castle

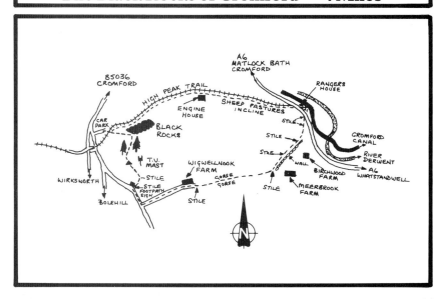

Cromford Wharf

CROMFORD CANAL — Originally 14½ miles long, it joined Arkwright's Cromford Mill with the Erewash Canal at Langley Mill. It was opened in 1793 and cost £80,000. At the nearby Wharf goods were transhipped to wagons and taken along the High Peak Railway line — a journey of two days.

THE BLACK ROCKS OF CROMFORD
4 Miles — Allow 2 hours

CAR PARK — Black Rocks picnic site.

MAPS — O.S. 1:25,000 Outdoor Leisure Map — The White Peak — East Sheet
O.S. 1:25,000 Pathfinder Series — Matlock (South) —
Sheet SK 25/35

ABOUT THE WALK — The Black Rocks provide a stunning vantage point over
the Matlock area. They are a popular climbing area surrounded by forest. First you
walk beneath the rocks along the High Peak Trail before descending to the High
Peak Junction, with the Cromford Canal. You then ascend across fields to gain the
summit of the Rocks before descending to the car park.

WALKING INSTRUCTIONS — From the car park make your way to the High
Peak Trail and turn left. You keep on the trail for the next 1½ miles, passing Sheep
Pastures Incline Engine House before descending to the High Peak Junction with
the Cromford Canal. Here, opposite the Rangers House, you turn right up a walled
path to the A6 road. Cross over to your left to a stile and follow the path, angling to
your left up the field to the wood. Here is another stile and cobbled path as you
continue ascending through Birch Wood. Cross another stile and now in open
country keep the wall on your left. Cross the track to Birchwood Farm on your right,
and continue to keep the wall on your left. Three fields later reach the track to
Meerbrook Farm. Turn right and follow this track for ½ mile to Wigwellnook Farm.
The track is well-stiled and passes through a gorse-lined section.

At the farm join the farm road and follow it to the minor road. Turn right and
descend towards the first house on your right, 200 yards away. Just before it, at the
stile and footpath sign, turn right and ascend to Black Rocks Plantation. Ascend the
stile and follow the wide path to your left, passing a prominent T.V. mast on your
right before reaching the white triangulation pillar and extensive view. Continue
along the path as it weaves its way through the trees and above old quarries on your
left. Keep to the path on your left to reach the summit of the Rocks before bearing
left down to the High Peak Trail and car park.

BLACK ROCKS — The view is extensive and is interesting geologically. You stand
on gritstone but down below can be seen large areas of limestone, noticeably the face
of High Tor.

HIGH PEAK TRAIL — A former railway with nine inclines that linked the
Cromford Canal with the Peak Forest Canal at Whaley Bridge, 33 miles away. The
line opened in 1830 and cost £180,000. Because of the nature of the terrain the line
was never a financial success, and by 1967 it was closed. In the 1970s a 17-mile
section from the canal to Dowlow near Buxton was converted to pedestrian use.

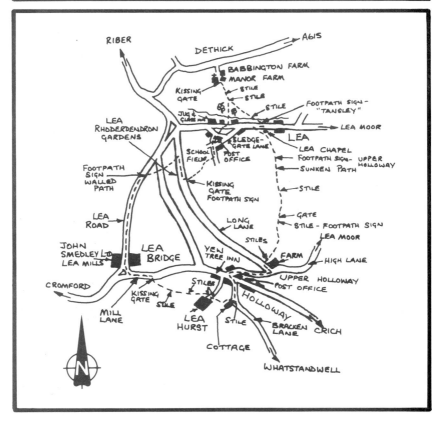

RIBER

DETHICK   A615

BABBINGTON FARM

MANOR FARM

KISSING   STILE
GATE   STILE

FOOTPATH SIGN —
"TANGLEY"

JUG &
GLASS INN   STILE

LEA MOOR

LEA
RHODDERDENDRON
GARDENS

LEA

SLEDGE-
GATE LANE

LEA CHAPEL

SCHOOL   POST
FIELD   OFFICE

FOOTPATH SIGN - UPPER
HOLLOWAY

SUNKEN PATH

FOOTPATH
SIGN
WALLED
PATH

KISSING
GATE
FOOTPATH SIGN

STILE

LEA
ROAD

LONG
LANE

GATE

STILE - FOOTPATH SIGN

STILES

LEA MOOR

JOHN
SMEDLEY LTD
LEA MILLS

LEA
BRIDGE

YEW
TREE INN

FARM

HIGH LANE

UPPER HOLLOWAY
POST OFFICE

CROMFORD

KISSING
GATE   STILE

STILES

HOLLOWAY

MILL
LANE

LEA
HURST

STILE

BRACKEN
LANE

CRICH

COTTAGE

WHATSTANDWELL

N

Lea Mill

LEA & DETHICK — 5 Miles
Allow 2½ hours

CAR PARK — No official car park. Parking is permissible in John Smedley Ltd's private car park at weekends only, for those visiting the High Peak Junction — ten minutes walk away.

MAPS — O.S. 1:25,000 Outdoor Leisure Map — The White Peak — East Sheet — O.S. 1:25,000 Pathfinder Series — Matlock (South) — Sheet SK 25/35

ABOUT THE WALK — You begin at an interesting mill complex before ascending through pine and rhododendrons to Lea Rhododendron Gardens, which make a June walk exceptionally attractive. You press on to Lea and more woodland to reach Dethick and its associations with the Babington family. Delightful field walking brings you to Holloway before walking beside Lea Hurst and its Florence Nightingale associations, back to Lea Mill.

WALKING INSTRUCTIONS — At Lea Bridge, turn right and walk along Lea Road, passing under a mill bridge. Keep on the road for the next ½ mile to a footpath sign and walled path on your right; ascend this. Cross the road to your left to the path on the left of Old Chapel House. The path winds its way through pine trees and rhododendrons to a minor road. Here turn right, passing the entrance to Lea Rhododendron Gardens on your right. 100 yards later leave the road at the footpath sign and kissing gate on your left. Follow this walled and fenced path around the school playing fields. Upon reaching a T-junction and path sign — "Holloway" — turn left. A short distance later cross Sledgegate Lane and continue ahead on the narrow road to another T-junction with Lea Post Office on your right. Cross the road to a small gate and follow the path on the right of the playing field. At the bottom reach another gate and path sign — "Wakebridge". Turn right, and 30 yards later left, at path sign and descend steps to a footbridge before ascending through woodland to a stile. Bear left around the edge of the field to another stile and across the next field to Dethick Church.

Retrace your steps back to the second stile. Instead of walking around the field edge on your right to the stile and woodland, keep more into the centre of the field, and over the brow you will see another stile into the woodland. Follow this path beyond as it angles down to another footbridge over the brook. Ascend to the road. Turn right and pass Lea Chapel on your left. Just beyond, as footpath-signposted — "Upper Holloway and Wakebridge" — turn left along the lane. At the end, as footpath signposted, bear right across the field to two stiles. Keep ahead to another and descend into a sunken hollow. Turn right and walk along this, passing a footpath sign — "Upper Holloway".
Later this becomes a walled path. Where the track turns sharp right, keep ahead to a stile and cross the field to a stile and footpath sign. Cross the next field to another stile and path sign, out of view just over the field brow. Descend beside the wall to Upper Holloway Farm. Keep ahead with the farm on your left using the stiles to gain

the road. Turn left then right and descend the lane to Holloway. Turn left, with the Post Office on your left, and turn right and walk along Bracken Lane. After 100 yards, where the road bears left and just in front of a cottage on your right, turn right over the stile and follow the distinct path to the field corner. Don't ascend the stile on your left — instead turn right along the field boundary to cross the drive to Lea Hurst. Follow the path round a high garden wall to another stile. Continue descending gently to another stile. Beyond you soon curve round to your right to a kissing gate and Mill Lane. Turn left and descend back to Lea Bridge.

LEA MILL — Formerly a cotton spinning mill belonging to the Nightingale family. Later changed to hosiery manufacture by Thomas Smedley. His son John modernised the mill and is renowned for his Smedley's Hydro, now the Council Offices in Matlock, and for Riber Castle, which he built in the second half of last century.

LEA RHODODENDRON GARDENS — Laid out by J.B. Marsden-Smedley and open to the public, to see the display of rhododendrons and azaleas, from Easter to mid-June.

JUG & GLASS INN — Dates from 1782 and was owned by the Nightingale family.

DETHICK — The hamlet is a jewel of the area and is sometimes called "The church in the farmyard". The church can be visited, and the key is obtained from the Dairy at Moor Farm. The prominent tower was built by Sir Anthony Babington in 1530; the weathered date stone can still be seen. Anthony Babington became immortalised by his attempts to release Mary Queen of Scots out of Wingfield Manor. This led to his execution at Lincoln in 1586. The 16th Century barn of Manor Farm bears the Coats of Arms of the Babington family.

LEA CHAPEL — dates from 1690.

"Lea Hurst" — House and Rose Garden

LEA HURST — is forever associated with Florence Nightingale, "The Lady with the Lamp". She was born in Florence, hence her Christian name. The house dates from the 17th Century, but in the 19th Century her father began enlarging the house. The date N1825 can be seen over the main doorway. After her magnificent work in the Crimea War, Florence made Lea Hurst her home, where she wrote numerous books on hospital organisations. She died on 13th August 1910. The house is now a residential home for the elderly.

St. Helen's Church, Churchtown

St. John's Chapel — Built in 1897 and designed by Sir Guy Dawber.

WALK RECORD CHART

Date
walked

DARLEY DALE — 4½ Miles...

TWO DALES & SYDNOPE — 4 Miles...

HALL DALE — 3 Miles ....

THREE VILLAGES — 4½ Miles...

THE RIVER DERWENT — 5 Miles...

BONSALL — 5 Miles..

MATLOCK'S ALPINE WALK — 5 Miles...

RIBER — 3½ Miles...

MATLOCK'S INDUSTRIAL PAST — 5 Miles.......................................

CROMFORD VILLAGE WALK — 3 Miles..

BLACK ROCKS OF CROMFORD — 4 Miles...

LEA & DETHICK — 5 Miles ....

THE JOHN MERRIL WALK BADGE — Walk six or more of these walks and
send details to John Merrill at J.N.M. PUBLICATIONS, enclosing £2.50 for a
special four colour embroidered badge and signed certificate.

*************** **YOU MAY PHOTOCOPY THIS PAGE** **************

Darley Bridge

34

OTHER BOOKS by John N. Merrill Published by J.N.M. PUBLICATIONS

CIRCULAR WALK GUIDES -
SHORT CIRCULAR WALKS IN THE PEAK DISTRICT
CIRCULAR WALKS IN WESTERN PEAKLAND
SHORT CIRCULAR WALKS IN THE STAFFORDSHIRE MOORLANDS
SHORT CIRCULAR WALKS AROUND THE TOWNS & VILLAGES OF THE PEAK DISTRICT
SHORT CIRCULAR WALKS AROUND MATLOCK
SHORT CIRCULAR WALKS IN THE DUKERIES
SHORT CIRCULAR WALKS IN SOUTH YORKSHIRE
SHORT CIRCULAR WALKS IN SOUTH DERBYSHIRE
SHORT CIRCULAR WALKS AROUND BUXTON
SHORT CIRCULAR WALKS IN THE HOPE VALLEY
40 SHORT CIRCULAR WALKS IN THE PEAK DISTRICT
CIRCULAR WALKS ON KINDER & BLEAKLOW
SHORT CIRCULAR WALKS IN SOUTH NOTTINGHAMSHIRE
SHIRT CIRCULAR WALKS IN CHESHIRE
SHORT CIRCULAR WALKS IN WEST YORKSHIRE
CIRCULAR WALKS TO PEAK DISTRICT AIRCRAFT WRECKS by J.Mason
CIRCULAR WALKS IN THE DERBYSHIRE DALES
SHORT CIRCULAR WALKS IN EAST DEVON
LONG CIRCULAR WALKS IN THE PEAK DISTRICT
LONG CIRCULAR WALKS IN THE STAFFORDSHIRE MOORLANDS

CANAL WALKS -
VOL 1 - DERBYSHIRE & NOTTINGHAMSHIRE
VOL 2 - CHESHIRE & STAFFORDSHIRE
VOL 3 - STAFFORDSHIRE
VOL 4 - THE CHESHIRE RING
VOL 5 - LINCOLNSHIRE & NOTTINGHAMSHIRE
VOL 6 - SOUTH YORKSHIRE
VOL 7 - THE TRENT & MERSEY CANAL

JOHN MERRILL DAY CHALLENGE WALKS -
WHITE PEAK CHALLENGE WALK
DARK PEAK CHALLENGE WALK
PEAK DISTRICT END TO END WALKS
STAFFORDSHIRE MOORLANDS CHALLENGE WALK
THE LITTLE JOHN CHALLENGE WALK
YORKSHIRE DALES CHALLENGE WALK
NORTH YORKSHIRE MOORS CHALLENGE WALK
LAKELAND CHALLENGE WALK
THE RUTLAND WATER CHALLENGE WALK
MALVERN HILLS CHALLENGE WALK
THE SALTER'S WAY
THE SNOWDONIA CHALLENGE

INSTRUCTION & RECORD -
HIKE TO BE FIT.....STROLLING WITH JOHN
THE JOHN MERRILL WALK RECORD BOOK

MULTIPLE DAY WALKS -
THE RIVERS'S WAY
PEAK DISTRICT: HIGH LEVEL ROUTE
PEAK DISTRICT MARATHONS
THE LIMEY WAY
THE PEAKLAND WAY

COAST WALKS & NATIONAL TRAILS -
ISLE OF WIGHT COAST PATH
PEMBROKESHIRE COAST PATH
THE CLEVELAND WAY

PEAK DISTRICT HISTORICAL GUIDES -
A to Z GUIDE OF THE PEAK DISTRICT
DERBYSHIRE INNS - an A to Z guide
HALLS AND CASTLES OF THE PEAK DISTRICT & DERBYSHIRE
TOURING THE PEAK DISTRICT & DERBYSHIRE BY CAR
DERBYSHIRE FOLKLORE
PUNISHMENT IN DERBYSHIRE
CUSTOMS OF THE PEAK DISTRICT & DERBYSHIRE
WINSTER - a souvenir guide
ARKWRIGHT OF CROMFORD
LEGENDS OF DERBYSHIRE
TALES FROM THE MINES by Geoffrey Carr
PEAK DISTRICT PLACE NAMES by Martin Spray

JOHN MERRILL'S MAJOR WALKS -
TURN RIGHT AT LAND'S END
WITH MUSTARD ON MY BACK
TURN RIGHT AT DEATH VALLEY
EMERALD COAST WALK

COLOUR GUIDES -
THE PEAK DISTRICT.........Something to remember her by.

SKETCH BOOKS -
NORTH STAFFORDSHIRE SKETCHBOOK by John Creber
SKETCHES OF THE PEAK DISTRICT

IN PREPARATION -
SHORT CIRCULAR WALKS IN THE YORKSHIRE DALES
SHORT CIRCULAR WALKS IN THE LAKE DISTRICT
SHORT CIRCULAR WALKS IN NORTH YORKSHIRE MOORS
CHARNWOOD FOREST CHALLENGE WALK
FOOTPATHS OF THE WORLD - Vol I - NORTH AMERICA
HIKING IN NEW MEXICO - 7 VOLUMES
Vol I - The Sandia and Manzano Mountains.

☞ Full list from JNM PUBLICATIONS, Winster,
Matlock, Derbyshire. DE4 2DQ